100 QUESTIONS about BIRDS

and all
the answers
too!

Written and Illustrated by
Simon Abbott

 PETER PAUPER PRESS, INC.
White Plains, New York

To Art

PETER PAUPER PRESS

In 1928, at the age of twenty-two, Peter Beilenson began printing books on a small press in the basement of his parents' home in Larchmont, New York. Peter—and later, his wife, Edna—sought to create fine books that sold at "prices even a pauper could afford."

Today, still family owned and operated, Peter Pauper Press continues to honor our founders' legacy of quality, value, and fun for big kids and small kids alike.

Designed by Heather Zschock

Text and illustrations copyright © 2022 by Simon Abbott

Published by Peter Pauper Press, Inc.
202 Mamaroneck Avenue
White Plains, New York 10601 USA

Published in the United Kingdom and Europe by Peter Pauper Press, Inc.
c/o White Pebble International
Unit 2, Plot 11 Terminus Rd.
Chichester, West Sussex PO19 8TX, UK

Library of Congress Cataloging-in-Publication Data Available

ISBN 978-1-4413-3812-9

Manufactured for Peter Pauper Press, Inc.
Printed in China

7 6 5 4 3 2 1

Visit us at www.peterpauper.com

Welcome to the wonderful world of birds!

Let's say hello to our feathery friends, and discover the secrets of the skies.

Why don't penguins fly?
How can a parrot talk?
What makes a flamingo pink?

Grab your binoculars and spot the answers to these questions, plus many more egg-citing facts. Get ready for take-off!

AVIAN ANCESTORS

Let's spread our wings and begin our exploration. Are you ready to get up close and personal with our planet's early birds?

When did birds first appear on Earth?

The oldest bird fossils date from the prehistoric Jurassic period, around 150 million years ago.

What did these ancient fossil birds look like?

Archaeopteryx (ahr-kee-OP-tuh-riks) is considered the first bird, and had some dinosaur features and some bird features. It was the size of a raven, with feathers, sharp teeth, three clawed fingers, and a long bony tail.

Archaeopteryx had dinosaur features? Are birds related to dinosaurs, then?

All birds are descended from a group of meat-eating dinosaurs called theropods. Dinosaurs are divided into two groups, with different hips: bird-hipped dinosaurs called ornithischians (awr-nuh-THIS-kee-uhns), and lizard-hipped specimens known as saurischians (saw-RIS-kee-uhns). Despite the name of the first group, Archaeopteryx and all other theropods actually belonged to the lizard-hipped second group!

SAURISCHIAN
Ilium
Pubis
Ischium

ORNITHISCHIANS
Ilium
Pubis
Ischium

What came after the dinosaur?

Its tail!

DEINONYCHUS

Which discovery gave scientists the idea that birds evolved from dinosaurs?

In the 1960s, scientists studied a theropod dinosaur called Deinonychus (day-NON-i-kuhs) and realized that it had several things in common with birds. It's believed that this clever, speedy dino was covered in feathers, and could glide or even fly with its wings. Other features some theropod dinos shared with birds include three-toed feet; light, hollow bones; and the furcula, or wishbone.

5

FEATHERED FAMILY TREE

The dinosaurs' reign on Earth is about to end with a bang. Who's waiting in the wings to take their place?

How were the dinosaurs wiped out?

Around 66 million years ago, a 9-mile (14 km) wide asteroid hit the Earth, kicking up enough debris to block out the sun and sparking forest fires with it. The planet got super hot, then entered a long sunless winter. Plants died, leaving the huge hungry dinosaurs without food. The dinos were wiped out.

Why did some early birds survive?

The birds that made it were small, and could adapt more easily. They could hide from fires or other disasters, and could survive on less food. They had beaks to crack open seeds and nuts from the burned-out forests, and peck at a variety of insects, fruit, and small animals. Through evolution, many birds became smaller, but kept their big brains. Their intelligence helped the birds survive, too!

So, the deadly dinosaurs are out of the picture. Which birds took over to rule the roost?

Let's hear it for the now extinct Phorusrhacids (fuhr-us-RASS-ids), otherwise known as terror birds, who flapped around South America from 62 to 2 million years ago.

Did they deserve their intimidating title?

I'll say! Take a look at their stats:

HEIGHT:	Up to 10 feet (3 m) tall. That's over one and a half times the length of your bed!
WEIGHT:	Up to 1,000 lbs (454 kg)
TOP SPEED:	30 to 60 mph (48–97 km/h) That's faster than a greyhound!
LOCATION:	South America (It was an island back then!)
WEAPONRY:	Rock-hard skull, deadly hooked beak, and four-toed feet with razor-sharp claws

Which ancient birds are still shaking a tail feather today?

It's believed that the **hoatzin** bird has been flying around our planet for over 36 million years. This resident of the Amazon basin is known as the stink bird, thanks to the food storage pouch near its throat. This pouch is filled with special bacteria to help the hoatzin digest leaves. Don't get too close, as it gives off the lovely aroma of manure!

FROM BEAK TO TAIL

It's time to take a look at a bird's amazing anatomy and find out how these fascinating creatures take flight.

What makes a bird a bird?
Let's look at the checklist:

- Birds are vertebrates: animals with backbones, like you.

- They're warm-blooded, which means they can keep their bodies at a particular temperature. (Just like you!)

- Their bodies are covered with feathers.

- They have light skeletons with hollow bones.

- They have toothless, beaked jaws.

- They hatch from eggs.

How do birds see the world?
Birds tend to have large eyes and first-class vision. Most birds' eyes point sideways to help them see more of the world around them. But some birds, such as owls, have forward-facing eyes. This helps them accurately judge how far away things are—a critical skill when hunting!

A bird's neck is incredibly flexible, and usually has twice as many neck bones as a mammal's. This allows birds to whip their heads every which way, giving them full view of their surroundings—important because their large eyes can't move much in their sockets!

EYE SOCKET

WRIST JOINT

ELBOW JOINT

FLEXIBLE NECK

TAKE A LOOK INSIDE!

KNEE JOINT   TOES

TAIL BONE

What is this odd-shaped bone?
This is the keel. It supports the super-strong flight muscles. Some flightless birds don't have this bone.

How many toes does a bird have?
Most have four toes. The typical bird has three toes pointing forward and one pointing back—a perfect arrangement for gripping a perch! Some birds, however, like to be different. Parrots, wood-peckers, toucans, and cuckoos all have two toes in the front and two in the back, which allow them to climb and grasp.

How can birds fly?

First, they need to be as light as possible. A bird's bones are hollow and filled with pockets of air. The bones' strength comes from thin bars inside each bone called **struts**. Birds also have lightweight beaks instead of heavy jaws and teeth, and their bodies are streamlined, allowing them to cut through the air with little resistance.

STREAMLINED SHAPE

BIRD'S HOLLOW BONE

STRUTS

How do their wings work?

Take a look at this side view. The wing is flat underneath and curved on top. Air passes faster above it than underneath, and this difference in speed creates a pocket of pressure under the wing that lifts the bird up. This is how an airplane takes off, too!

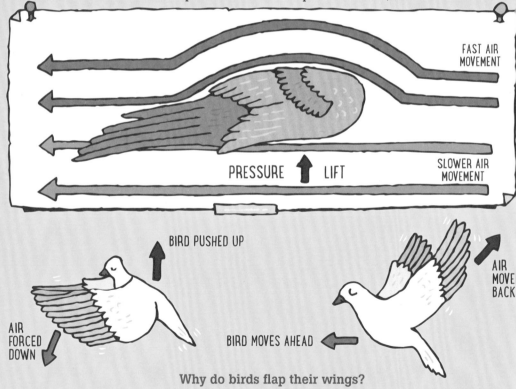

FAST AIR MOVEMENT

SLOWER AIR MOVEMENT

PRESSURE LIFT

BIRD PUSHED UP

AIR MOVE BACK

AIR FORCED DOWN

BIRD MOVES AHEAD

Why do birds flap their wings?

As the wing flaps downward, air is forced down, and the bird is pushed up. The wing tip angles forward to move the air back, and the bird moves ahead. Then the wing moves right back to the start to flap again.

How does a flying bird change direction?

It changes the shape or angle of its wings. If it dips
one wing down, it turns to that side.

How did the injured bird land safely?

It used a sparrow-chute!

How can a bird land, or slow down?

It can fan out its tail feathers, and angle its
wings back. This creates air resistance,
which slows the bird down.

Can a bird fly backward?

Most birds can't really, but **hummingbirds** can! These tiny
birds have a unique ball and socket joint at their shoulder,
which lets them rotate their wings 180 degrees in all directions.
They can flap their wings up to 100 times a second when
they've eaten their fill of sugary, energy-rich nectar!

EGG-CELLENT WORK!

Let's fly by and look at the beginning of a baby bird's life. Get ready to meet the new kids on the branch!

How do baby birds begin their time on Earth?

First things first: A parent bird needs to attract a mate. This may involve dramatic flight displays, wing or tail beating, dancing, bird song, or simply fancy colorful feathers. The male bird fertilizes the egg within the female, which she lays in a nest. How many eggs a female lays can vary from species to species. Some only lay one, while others can lay dozens. (The gray partridge lays the most, with up to 22 eggs!) This egg collection is called a clutch.

How does the chick develop?

The egg must stay warm to survive, so a parent bird will usually sit on its eggs to keep them toasty. This is known as **incubation**. The egg contains **albumen** (egg white) and a yolk. The embryo inside the egg can feed off the yolk and egg white until it is ready to hatch. Most birds have a bump, or egg tooth, on the tip of their beak, which they use to break out of their eggs. This tooth usually disappears a few weeks post-hatching.

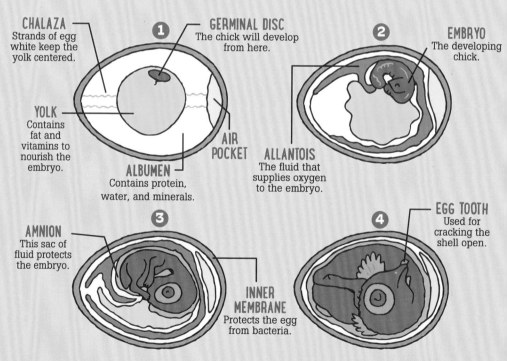

CHALAZA
Strands of egg white keep the yolk centered.

① GERMINAL DISC
The chick will develop from here.

② EMBRYO
The developing chick.

YOLK
Contains fat and vitamins to nourish the embryo.

AIR POCKET

ALLANTOIS
The fluid that supplies oxygen to the embryo.

ALBUMEN
Contains protein, water, and minerals.

AMNION
This sac of fluid protects the embryo.

③

INNER MEMBRANE
Protects the egg from bacteria.

④

EGG TOOTH
Used for cracking the shell open.

How long does incubation last?

Large birds lay large eggs, which take much longer to hatch. A dove will sit on its eggs for 14 days, but an emu chick can take up to 56 days to hatch.

What do birds build their nests from?

Different birds find different materials and locations. Ringed plovers make a shallow scrape on a beach, orioles weave incredible hanging nests, guillemots (seabirds) take shelter on seaside cliffs, and many owls find a hole in a tree. Swallows find mud to stick their straw nests together, European goldfinches will "glue" their nests to a branch with sticky threads from spiderwebs, and edible-nest swiftlets make cliffside nests from layers of their own saliva!

That sounds exhausting! Are all birds this industrious?

No! Some cuckoos don't bother to build a nest. They simply lay their eggs in another bird's nest: a warbler, for example. When the cuckoo chick hatches, it boots out the warbler eggs, then hangs around to be fed by the parent warbler until it's old enough to fly.

Is it always the female bird that incubates the eggs?

Not always! A female **emperor penguin** lays a single egg in May or June, then leaves on a two-month hunting trip. It's up to the male penguin to protect the egg from the freezing Antarctic weather. He balances the egg on his feet, then covers it with a feathery layer of skin called the brood pouch. Cozy!

TWEET TWEET!

Birds make more complex sounds than any other animal. Let's find out why they call, sing, chirp, cheep, and tweet!

How do birds make their distinctive sounds?

It's thanks to a vocal organ called the **syrinx** (SIR-inks). The two sides of this voice box work independently, letting a bird create more than one sound at once, and control the volume and complexity of the call.

Why do birds sing?

To show off! Birds tend to sing the most during the warm spring and summer months, when they're trying to find a mate. The "dawn chorus" can start as early as 4 AM. The strongest male birds usually make the most noise. Their songs demonstrate their strength to potential partners . . . and to anyone who thinks about invading their territories.

So, calls are used to attract a mate. Why else do birds communicate?

- Birds use loud, short sounds to warn of danger.

- Young birds call and flap their wings to get their parents' attention.

- Flocks of birds "call" each other mid-flight to check in with each other, or to pass on information.

- Birds use song to stake a claim on a territory, and warn other rival birds to keep clear.

Which bird has the loudest call?
That record is held by the **white bellbird**. At a volume of 125 decibels, this noisy specimen is louder than an ambulance siren!

When's the best time to buy a parrot?

When they're going cheep!

Can birds copy the human voice?
Crows, mynah birds, ravens, starlings, mockingbirds, and others all can copy sounds that they hear. The expert imitators, however, are parrots, with one talented parakeet having a vocabulary of around 1,728 words!

How do they do that, and why?
Most songbirds learn songs from other birds using a part of their brain called the song system. Scientists have discovered that parrots have an extra part of this system, which could be the key to their mimicking skill. Parrots are also sociable. As pets, they copy words in order to fit in with their human family.

15

READY FOR TAKE-OFF!

Around one-third of all birds make an extraordinarily long journey called a migration. Let's find out why!

Which birds migrate?

Around 4,000 species of birds migrate. Non-migrant, or sedentary, birds such as blue jays and northern cardinals stay near one location all year-round, to defend their territory, to bring up their young, or because migrating requires a lot of energy that birds would rather spend on other things, such as foraging or escaping predators.

Why do migratory birds risk such a hazardous journey, and expose themselves to storms, starvation, predators, and loss of habitat?

Most travel in search of food or a good nesting spot. Long-distance migrants, such as **Canada geese**, fly south to escape the freezing North American winters. The willow warbler, one of the world's smallest migrating birds, travels 5,000 miles (8,000 km) from Africa to Europe and northern Asia each spring, arriving in time to snack on the never-ending supply of insects.

Why do birds fly south in the winter?

Because it's too far to walk!

Why doesn't the willow warbler stay in Africa all year?

Migration is about survival. This tiny, 5-inch (12.5 cm) bird flies all the way back north for the summer because:

- There are fewer birds up north, so it has less competition for nest sites.

- It can enjoy a constant supply of insects in the warm, wet summer months.

- Europe and northern Asia get more hours of daylight than Africa in summer. The longer days give parent birds extra time to feed their young.

- It has fewer predators up north.

Do migrating birds fly nonstop?

Some do! A bar-tailed godwit made the longest recorded nonstop flight in 2020, clocking an impressive 7,500 miles (12,000 km) en route from Alaska to New Zealand. When migrating from Europe to Africa, however, some wading birds avoid crossing the Sahara Desert (which is as big as the mainland U.S.) and follow the coastal route instead. This allows them to make food stops in waters along the way.

How do migrating birds know which direction to fly in?

We're not exactly sure! They can use the position of the sun, moon, and stars, and take advantage of a built-in "GPS system" using the Earth's magnetic field. In experiments, when birds were moved 1,500 miles (2,414 km) from their habitat before the migration season, they still managed to retrace their regular migratory path. Birds prepare for the long journey by fueling up with high energy foods. For instance, before heading south, semipalmated sandpipers stop off at the Bay of Fundy in Canada to guzzle mud shrimp. Some double their body mass in just two weeks!

SOARING SUPERSTARS!

Let's swoop by some gliding gold-medalists, and take a trip to the High–Flying Hall of Fame!

Which bird gets the Widest Wingspan Award?
The wandering albatross has the largest wingspan of any bird. It stretches up to an incredible 12 feet (3.66 m), which is almost twice as long as your bed!

Let's go to the other end of the scale.
Which bird wins the Miniature Medal?
The bee hummingbird measures just over 2 inches (51 mm),
and weighs about the same as a paper clip!

Which speedy star grabs the Fastest Flier Cup?

The hunting dive of the **peregrine falcon** reaches astonishing speeds of over 200 mph (320 km/h). That makes it the fastest animal on Earth! Outside of a dive, the award for fastest flier goes to the super-speedy spine-tailed swift, with a remarkable top speed of 106 mph (171 km/h). That's faster than a cheetah!

Which first-class flier has reached dizzying heights?

The **bar-headed goose** can fly over the world's tallest mountain range in just eight hours. This Himalayan resident can soar to a height of almost 21,120 feet (6,437 m). That's almost 17 Empire State Buildings on top of each other!

Which bird wins the World's Best Mom award?
The largest egg ever recorded was laid by an **ostrich**, and tipped the scales at 5 lb, 11 oz (2.589 kg). That's heavier than three and a half basketballs. The Egg-cellent Egg Layer trophy goes to an anonymous **White Leghorn** hen, who generated 371 eggs in 364 days! Egg-cellent work!

Who's in line for the Housebuilding Honor?
Let's hear it for a pair of **bald eagles** from Florida who put together a nest measuring 9.5 feet (2.9 m) wide and weighing over 2 tons. That's as heavy as a rhinoceros!

**Which skillful specimen has clawed its way
to the top of the Brainy Bird League?**

Three cheers for the humble **crow**, one of the most intelligent creatures on Earth. This bird can solve problems, use tools, plan ahead, make connections between objects or concepts, and recall human faces.

What do you get if you cross a messenger pigeon with a parrot?

A bird that delivers voice mail!

Which heroic flyer wins the Brave Bird Prize?
In World War II, a British bomber plane was hit by enemy fire and crashed into the freezing North Sea. The crew was unable to radio for help, so they released Winkie, their **carrier pigeon**, in the hope that she would fly back to the air base and alert their colleagues. After an exhausting 120-mile (193 km) flight, Winkie's return triggered a rescue mission, and the men were saved. Winkie then became the first animal awarded the Dickin Medal for delivering a message under exceptional difficulties.

ON THE HUNT

Let's meet some powerful birds of prey, and see how these creatures track and snare their meals!

What sets birds of prey apart from other kinds of birds?

These creatures are excellent hunters. They attack their prey with sharp, curved claws, then tear it apart with their hook-tipped beaks. They have superb long-distance vision. Bald eagles can see eight times farther than you or me!

How many types of birds of prey are there?

Birds of prey fall into three main groups:

Accipitriformes: There are over 250 species in this group, including hawks, eagles, vultures, ospreys, and more. These animals are diurnal, which means they hunt during the day.

Falconiformes: This group includes around 60 species of falcons (like the super-speedy peregrine on page 19) and bald-faced birds called caracaras. They look a lot like hawks, but scientists have found they're more closely related to parrots and songbirds!

Strigiformes: This group contains over 200 species of owls. Most of these birds are nocturnal, so they catch their prey at night.

Let's take a look at some stand-out specimens:

HARPY EAGLE

How big is it?
Males weigh about 8.5 to 12 pounds (3.9 to 5.4 kg), but females are much larger, at 14 to 20 pounds (6.4 to 9 kg). Harpy eagles are equipped with back talons longer than a grizzly bear's claws!

Where does it live?
In forests from Mexico to northern Argentina.

What does it eat?
It catches porcupines, snakes, iguanas, and opossums, and grabs sloths and monkeys from branches in the rainforest.

RUPPELL'S GRIFFON VULTURE

How big is it?
These powerful birds have an 8-foot (2.5 m) wingspan. That's longer than two baseball bats end to end!

Where does it live?
In the mountains of Africa.

How does it hunt for food?
This vulture can stay airborne for up to seven hours a day, and uses its first-class eyesight to spot a carcass on the ground below. It sometimes climbs inside the dead animal's rib cage to begin the feast!

OSPREY

How big is it?
An adult osprey is about 1.75 to 2 feet (0.5 to 0.6 m) tall. That's as tall as a four-month-old baby!

What does it eat?
About 99 percent of its diet is made up of fish. It dives to the surface of the water and grabs a fish with its curved claws. The osprey holds on to the catch using the gripping pads on its feet, and points the fish headfirst for less resistance as it flies away.

Where does the osprey live?
It can be found near rivers, lakes, and ponds in every continent except Antarctica.

BALD EAGLE

How fast and how high can it fly?

When diving for prey, the bald eagle can reach speeds of 100 mph (160 km/h). It can soar up to 10,000 feet (3,000 m) high. That's twice the height of Mount Rushmore!

What does it hunt?

Bald eagles usually live near a water source, so they search out fish, ducks, snakes, and turtles.

What's the bald eagle's secret weapon?

Its eye has two focal points, which means it can look ahead and to the side at the same time. You try doing that!

GREAT HORNED OWL

How big is it?

It's about 1.5 to 2 feet (0.4 to 0.6 m) tall, with a wingspan about 3.3 to 4.8 feet (1 to 1.5 m) wide. That's about as tall as 4 soda cans, and almost as wide as a bathtub is long!

What does the great horned owl hunt?

This powerful predator feasts on practically anything it can catch, including skunks, rabbits, squirrels, raccoons, other owls, and even occasional dogs or cats! Like most other owls, the great horned owl swallows its prey whole, then coughs up a pellet of the parts it can't digest, such as hair and bones.

Where does it live?

North and South America, and the Arctic.

RED KITE

How large is this bird of prey?
Despite an impressive wingspan of almost 6 feet (1.7 m), this lightweight raptor weighs only around 2 to 3 pounds (1 to 1.3 kg). That's as heavy as a human brain!

What is its most distinctive feature?
The red kite has a unique forked tail, which it uses to steer and change direction mid-flight.

How common are red kites?
This bird of prey lives in woodlands, wetlands, and valleys throughout Europe. Some also nest in Morocco. A century ago, only two known pairs of red kites survived in the U.K. After an intensive protection program, there are now more than 1,800 breeding pairs!

RED-TAILED HAWK

How big is this raptor?
This red-hued raptor is the largest hawk, with a wingspan roughly nine times wider than this book! Like most raptors, the female is almost a third larger than the male.

What does the red-tailed hawk eat?
Around 90 percent of its diet is small rodents. It hunts in open spaces such as deserts and fields.

How do red-tailed hawks attract a mate?
A pair of courting hawks flies in huge circles at great heights, before the male makes a deep dive. When the male soars back up to return to the female, they'll grasp each other with their sharp talons, then spiral down together toward the ground. How romantic!

YOU'RE GROUNDED!

Believe it or not, some birds can't fly! Let's get the data on these land-based specimens.

Why are some birds flightless?
Scientists think that through evolution, these birds lost the ability to fly. Their ancestors may have lived in places without predators, so they had no need to flap their wings and escape. One group of flightless birds, called ratites, are also missing the keel, which is the bone that flight muscles are attached to.

Has the keel disappeared in all flightless birds?
In penguins, the keel and flight muscles remain, but the wings have evolved to become paddles for swimming. These paddles allow the gentoo penguin to reach underwater speeds of 22 mph (35 km/h), faster than any other diving bird can swim.

How have flightless birds adapted and survived?
Take a look at the birds ahead to find out!

How does the ostrich get around?
It can sprint at up to 43 mph (69 km/h), and can change direction using its wings as rudders. It kicks out at predators with its super-strong legs. When it's not dashing and kicking, it gorges on a diet of plants, roots, seeds, and insects—all of which are plentiful in its African savanna home.

How can the cassowary defend itself?

Don't pick a fight with this species. It's been named the most dangerous bird in the world! The cassowary weighs almost 100 pounds (45 kg). It attacks its opponent by kicking viciously with sets of 4-inch (10 cm) razor-sharp claws.

How does the Galapagos cormorant catch its dinner?

Unlike other cormorants, the Galapagos cormorant has tiny flightless wings, but that doesn't slow it down. This seafaring creature dives to the ocean floor to hunt for eel and octopus. It kicks back its powerful legs and snatches its prey with the help of its forceful, flexible neck.

What do you call a happy penguin?

A pen-grin!

Do flightless birds migrate?

Migration isn't just for flying birds. The **Adélie penguin** waddles 8,000 miles (13,000 km) across the freezing Antarctic every year. Why? Because for months each winter, parts of Antarctica plunge into 24-hour night. The penguins are following the sun!

What's unique about the kiwi?

This New Zealand native is the only bird in the world to have nostrils at the end of its beak. These nostrils help the bird sniff out worms (its favorite snack), bugs, and seeds when it pokes underground for food. The kiwi can't see well, so whiskers near its beak help the bird avoid bumping into obstacles in the dark.

SPECTACULAR SEABIRDS

Let's take a trip to the coast, and meet the birds that have swimming, diving, and fishing on their to-do list.

How do birds adapt to life by the sea?

- Flexible webbed feet help birds swim fast, and propel them out of the water when they take flight.

- Many seabirds have salt glands, which filter out salt and allow them to drink seawater without getting dehydrated.

- Seabirds' wings have adapted to their ocean habitat. The Arctic tern uses its long, pointed wings to glide over water and scoop up fish without spending too much energy. The terns' wings also let them fly long distances to sunlit places (where it's easier to see fish!) while their Arctic homes experience long, dark winters. The puffin's wings, meanwhile, are short and strong, giving it greater control when it dives underwater for fish.

- Instead of building nests in trees, some seabirds like kittiwakes, guillemots, and gannets shelter their eggs in rocky seaside cliffs.

- Seabirds are covered in waterproof feathers, which help them float and keep them warm in chilly sea conditions.

What do you call a man with a kittiwake on his head?

Cliff!

How do seabirds cope with the sun's glare on the water?
Some have built-in sunglasses! Their eyes can filter out the sun's UV light, protecting their vision and helping them see fish beneath the water's surface.

Shall we take a look at some stellar seabirds?

ATLANTIC PUFFIN

What stands out about this seabird?
This super-strong swimmer sports a colorful beak in springtime, which fades to dull grayish hues in winter. It's thought that the flashy beak helps puffins attract mates!

AUSTRALIAN PELICAN

How does this seabird catch its dinner?
It uses its pouch-like beak, which, when expanded, can hold almost 3 gallons (13 liters). The pelican plunges its beak into the water, and its pouch acts as a net. Once it catches a fish, the bird drains the water from its beak, then swallows its prey whole with a jerk of its head.

BLUE-FOOTED BOOBY

Why are these birds' feet bright blue?
That blue comes from the bird's anchovy-rich diet, but the azure hue is useful to this flashy species! When trying to attract a mate, the males perform a high-stepping swagger to show off their amazing feet. The bluer a booby's feet, the more attention he'll get!

DOUBLE-CRESTED CORMORANT

What makes this high-flyer a fantastic fisher?
The cormorant doesn't just dive like an Arctic tern; it also chases fish in the water at high speeds like a puffin! When it catches a crab or a crayfish, this bird batters its prey on the water to shake off the animal's legs, tosses it in the air, then catches it headfirst before gulping it down!

GREAT BLACK-BACKED GULL

What's notable about this splendid seabird?
It's the largest gull in the world, with a wingspan between 5 and 5.5 feet (1.5 and 1.7 m) wide! These powerful birds aren't picky eaters and will dine on fish, crustaceans, insects, small birds, eggs, rats, mice, and rabbits.

CRESTED AUKLET

How can I spot this seabird?

You'll probably hear them first! The crested auklet's breeding colonies are rowdy places, with birds honking, grunting, peeping, and whistling. You might smell them, too! Crested auklets emit a lemony-orange scent through their neck feathers in order to attract mates.

LEAST STORM PETREL

What is this breed's claim to fame?

The least storm petrel is one of the smallest seabirds, at 6 inches (15 cm) tall. They can scoop up small crustaceans and plankton from the surface of the sea without getting their feathers wet!

PERFECT BALANCE

Over half of all bird species are perching birds. Let's land and get the low-down on these tree-loving tweeters!

How many species does this group cover?
There are about 6,500 species in the perching bird, or passerine, group. It's divided into three sub-groups:

Tyranni
The 1,000-plus species in this group can be found across the world, though most live in South America. Tyranni includes woodcreepers, antbirds, and flycatchers, among others.

Passeri
The thousands of species in Passeri are often called songbirds, as their vocal organs allow them to make a variety of sounds. Sparrows, jays, finches, wrens, and many others are all members of this group.

Acanthisitti
This is a small, ancient group of birds found only in New Zealand. Just two species survive today.

Do these groups of passerines have things in common?
As you'd expect, perching birds have a special foot for holding branches (in other words, perching), with one toe facing backward and three toes pointing forward. Their sharp claws are curved, and they have a tendon at the back of their leg which automatically tightens and pulls whenever the leg is bent. This means they can sleep while perched in a tree, and not fall!

If they perch in trees, how big can passerines get?
The largest passerine is the **thick-billed raven**, which weighs about 2.5 to
3.3 pounds (1.13 to 1.5 kg) and stands nearly three times the height of this book!
At the other end of the scale is the **short-tailed pygmy tyrant**. This teeny tweeter
is a mere 2.6 inches (6.6 cm) tall and weighs only 0.14 ounces (4.2 g). That
means it weighs less than a grape!

Which perching bird is the longest?
The **ribbon-tailed astrapia** claims that title. Its body is a modest
12.5 inches (32 cm), but the male's tail tacks on an additional 37 inches
(94 cm), making it a whopping 4.1 feet (1.2 m) long from tip to tail!

Do passerines make good pets?

Sure! Budgerigars, also known as budgies or parakeets, are good-natured and smart. They are happy to sing and whistle, and some superb specimens can learn words and phrases. Other potential house birds include the chatty cockatiel, the friendly finch, or the delightful dove.

Which birds are famous for their beautiful songs?

Some of the top contenders include the wood thrush, the veery, and the common loon. Famed ornithologist Frank M. Chapman named the slate-colored solitaire as the bird world's singing superstar! Which is your favorite?

Just how soothing are passerine songs?

Very soothing! Scientists have found that humans feel more relaxed and focused when they hear birdsong (which, of course, mostly comes from passerine birds). Listening to recorded birdsong can help people get things done. Birdsong is sometimes piped into crowded places, such as Amsterdam's Schiphol Airport, to calm people passing through hectic, busy areas.

Which passerine birds are the biggest?

Corvids (or the crow family) grow the largest of all perching birds. These giant songbirds include rooks, ravens, crows, jays, magpies, and jackdaws. They are remarkably intelligent, and have a brain-to-body ratio equal to a great ape.

Which perching bird tries to fight itself?

The male cardinal is extremely territorial, and will defend its nest at all costs. It will sometimes try to attack its own reflection, and charge head-first into a window to fight its reflected "enemy." Ouch!

TREETOP TWEETERS

Time to turn over a new leaf and head to the woods. Which birds will we find there?

Isn't it difficult to fly through dense woodland?
Not if you're built for agility! Take the **sharp-skinned hawk**, for example. With its short wings and long tail, this rapid-flying raptor can shoot around tree branches and trunks with both speed and precision.

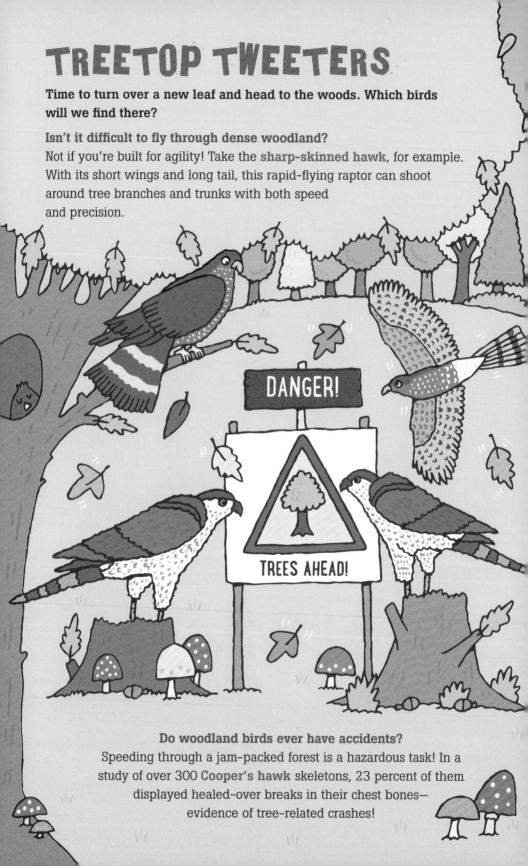

DANGER!

TREES AHEAD!

Do woodland birds ever have accidents?
Speeding through a jam-packed forest is a hazardous task! In a study of over 300 **Cooper's hawk** skeletons, 23 percent of them displayed healed-over breaks in their chest bones—evidence of tree-related crashes!

How do birds establish a territory in crowded woodlands?
Many woodpeckers tap on trees with their beaks to make their authority known, and to impress a potential mate. This high-speed drumming would give an ordinary bird a headache, but the front of a woodpecker's skull is made of a spongy material called the cancellous bone, which absorbs the shock of impact.

SPONGY CANCELLOUS BONE

How do woodland birds hide from predators?
With its brown, mottled feathers, the great potoo is the world expert in imitating a tree trunk! This camouflaged specimen is almost 2 feet (0.6 m) tall, and can sit undetected for hours, even while snatching beetles and moths from the air!

RHINOCEROS HORNBILL

Why does it have a double beak?
The horn atop this bird's head is a hollow structure called a casque, and is made of a material called keratin. (Your fingernails are made from keratin, too!) It's thought that the casque acts as a megaphone, to increase the volume of the male hornbill's mating signal.

Where does it live?
The rhinoceros hornbill lives in tropical rainforests in Southeast Asia. It feeds on fruit, with the occasional nibble on an insect or small animal.

EUROPEAN NIGHTJAR

What makes these birds unusual?
The male has a unique churring call, which can feature around 1,900 notes per minute. How many notes per minute can you sing?

How does the male charm the female nightjar?
He impresses a potential mate with a behavior called wing clapping. When in flight, the male nightjar flaps his wings with a sharp snap, which sounds like the cracking of a whip.

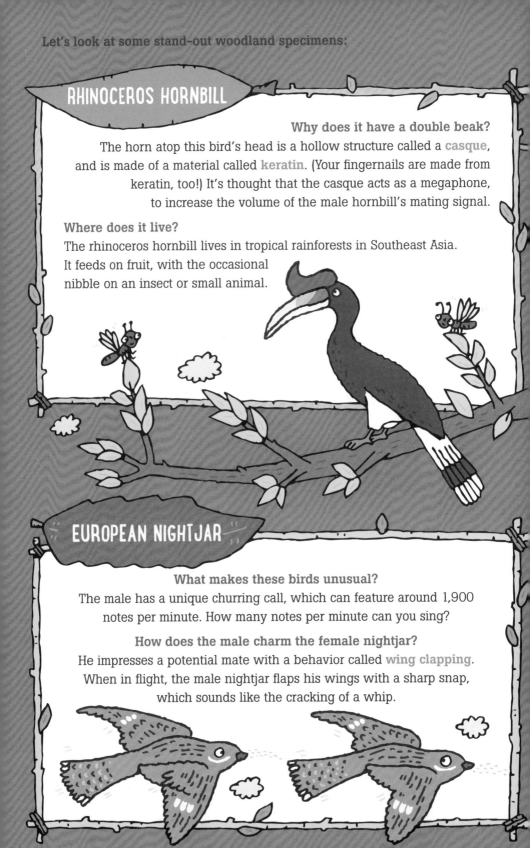

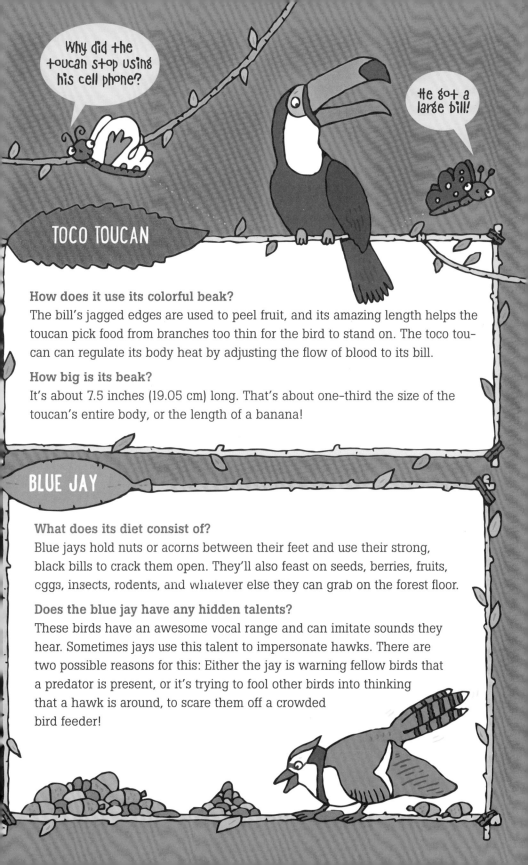

Why did the toucan stop using his cell phone?

He got a large bill!

TOCO TOUCAN

How does it use its colorful beak?
The bill's jagged edges are used to peel fruit, and its amazing length helps the toucan pick food from branches too thin for the bird to stand on. The toco toucan can regulate its body heat by adjusting the flow of blood to its bill.

How big is its beak?
It's about 7.5 inches (19.05 cm) long. That's about one-third the size of the toucan's entire body, or the length of a banana!

BLUE JAY

What does its diet consist of?
Blue jays hold nuts or acorns between their feet and use their strong, black bills to crack them open. They'll also feast on seeds, berries, fruits, eggs, insects, rodents, and whatever else they can grab on the forest floor.

Does the blue jay have any hidden talents?
These birds have an awesome vocal range and can imitate sounds they hear. Sometimes jays use this talent to impersonate hawks. There are two possible reasons for this: Either the jay is warning fellow birds that a predator is present, or it's trying to fool other birds into thinking that a hawk is around, to scare them off a crowded bird feeder!

MAKING A SPLASH

Let's leave the forest behind, and dip our toes into a lake, pond, river, or marsh! It's time to get the facts and figures on birds that wade and waddle in water.

How have these birds adapted to their environment?
Take a look!

Legs and feet
Ducks, geese, swans, and many other swimming birds have webbed feet for paddling through water and walking on soft mud. A heron can use its long legs to wade out into deep water and catch fish.

> What did the duck say when the waitress brought the check?

> "Please put it on my bill!"

Feathers
Most birds have a preen gland in their tails. This gland gives off an oil that the bird can spread all over its body to make its feathers waterproof.

Beaks
Some wading birds, like the **curlew**, use their extra-long beaks like chopsticks to pick at worms buried deep in the mud while keeping their heads out of the water. At the other end of the scale, a **lapwing** has a shorter beak, so it snaps at insects on the surface of the water.

Do all freshwater birds pinch, peck, and jab at their food like the curlew does? Water birds have lots of different beak shapes, and catch their food in all kinds of ways. Some birds, such as **flamingos**, are filter feeders. They have a wide, bent beak lined with rows of tiny horned plates. The bird swings its head from side to side and uses its tongue to pump the water around as the horned plates strain tiny, tasty creatures and plants from the water.

How do birds float and dive?

Let's take the **duck** as an example:

1. The duck's feathers are tightly linked in a way that traps air, making the bird extra buoyant. When the duck is ready to plunge underwater, it simply squeezes its feathers against its body and presses out the air.

2. A duck has a series of air sacs, including its lungs, along the length of its body. These help keep the bird afloat.

3. Like most birds, ducks have hollow bones. This makes them light and buoyant.

SPOONBILL

How big is this bird?
The spoonbill reaches about 2.5 feet (0.8 m) in height. That's almost as tall as a stove!

How does the spoonbill feed?
Its rounded, "spoon-shaped" bill is loaded with nerves that detect tiny vibrations from insects, worms, crustaceans, fish, and frogs. It swings its slightly open beak from side to side through the water, and strains out its prey from the muddy depths.

FLAMINGO

Why is the flamingo pink?
A flamingo is born gray, but its feathers change to their unique pink color when the bird is around two years old. They get their pink hue from a pigment in the algae, larvae, and shrimp that the flamingo feasts on. As they say, you are what you eat!

Are these birds sociable?
The lesser flamingo lives in the largest flocks, some of which contain hundreds of birds!

MANDARIN DUCK

Why does this bird stand out?
The male mandarin is famous for its multicolored plumage. It sports an eye-catching crest of black, green, blue, and copper, a purple breast, golden wings, and a red beak. However, when it molts (sheds its feathers and grows new ones) after mating season, its feathers turn to dull gray and brown.

Do mandarin ducks make good parents?
It's mostly up to the mama duck. She lays her eggs in a tree hollow about 30 feet (9 m) from the ground. The male helps out with nest defense, but usually heads off before the chicks hatch. After hatching, the still-flightless young chicks must leap to the ground, under the watchful eye of their mom, with a cushion of leaves and grass to break their fall!

TRUMPETER SWAN

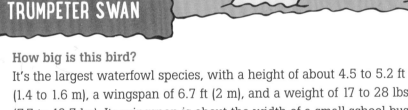

How big is this bird?
It's the largest waterfowl species, with a height of about 4.5 to 5.2 ft (1.4 to 1.6 m), a wingspan of 6.7 ft (2 m), and a weight of 17 to 28 lbs (7.7 to 12.7 kg). Its wingspan is about the width of a small school bus, and it's as heavy as two bowling balls!

How long do these birds live?
In the wild, trumpeter swans can live for over 20 years. Like all swans, they mate for life. The female lays three to eight eggs each breeding season in nest mounds made from reeds, grasses, and cattails.

BYE, BYE, BIRDY!

Over the past 500 years, over 190 species of birds have become extinct. Let's find out why!

What can cause birds to go extinct?

One in eight bird species is currently in danger of extinction. They face similar threats to those that killed the dodo, the passenger pigeon, and other birds driven to extinction in the past:

- Much of the world's food is grown using industrial farming methods that destroy bird habitats and use pesticides that are toxic to some birds.

- More birds live in forests than in any other habitat. The global demand for timber, and the destruction of forests to provide grazing for cattle and space for crops, has devastated bird habitats.

- Invasive species such as rats and mice, usually introduced by humans, are responsible for over 70 percent of bird extinctions. Birds on remote islands are particularly vulnerable to this threat. They often don't have many natural predators, and can't protect themselves.

- When people hunt and capture rare bird species, their populations can quickly collapse.

- Climate change affects birds across the world. They're struggling to keep up with radical differences in the weather, seasons, their food, when they can nest, and more.

Let's pay tribute to some impressive birds that no longer inhabit our planet:

What's the opposite of a dodo bird?

A don't don't bird!

DODO

Why did it become extinct?

The last dodo was killed in 1681. Portuguese sailors first happened upon these birds in 1507, on an island in the Indian Ocean called Mauritius. The sailors hunted dodos to supplement their meat rations on long voyages. They also brought in pigs and monkeys that ate the dodos' eggs and wiped out their food supply.

THE PASSENGER PIGEON

How did this species reach its end?
At one time, this was the most abundant bird in North America, with a population of well over three billion. Passenger pigeon numbers began to decline in 1800, due to mass hunting and deforestation. Because these birds relied on their large flocks for survival, as more and more birds were killed, it became harder for the remaining birds to keep going. Martha, the last known passenger pigeon, died at the Cincinnati Zoo in 1914.

THE ELEPHANT BIRD

Were these birds as big as they sound?
This ostrich-like animal weighed about half a ton and was almost 10 feet (3 m) tall—taller than an Asian elephant! Although it died out around 1,400 years ago, we can posthumously hand this flightless creature the World's Tallest Bird award.

How did this behemoth bird die out?
Scientists aren't sure, but there are two leading theories. First, the climate may have shifted on its own long, long ago, and the bird couldn't adapt. Or, its numbers may have dwindled when humans arrived on its island home thousands of years ago. The humans might have hunted elephant birds, destroyed their habitats, or introduced other birds that passed new diseases to them.

THE STEPHENS ISLAND WREN

What was the fate of this tiny, flightless bird?
This semi-nocturnal creature once hopped around all of New Zealand, but by 1894, a combination of habitat destruction and the introduction of cats and rats had nearly wiped out its entire population, leaving just a small flock on Stephens Island. That was until a pregnant cat named Tibbles escaped from the island's lighthouse. Now, I'm not saying that Tibbles or her litter were entirely responsible. But in just a short space of time, the Stephens Island wren was a thing of the past!

HOME TWEET HOME!

Let's get closer to home and explore the bird life in our own backyard!

How can I attract more birds to my garden?

Birds need to feel safe in a space where they can socialize. Food, water, and shelter are essential. The best way to bring in birds is to grow native plants that will feed or shelter them. Search online for bird-friendly plants native to your area! You can also put up a bird feeder.

Where should I place my bird feeder?

If possible, put up a few feeders in different locations. Finches and nuthatches are happy to hold on to hanging feeders (with small holes for small beaks). Cardinals and blue jays like hopper feeders (feeders that dispense feed into a tray) or tray feeders (open trays hung from trees). Some birds will glide straight onto an exposed perch, but others prefer a feeder with some natural cover. Clean your feeders regularly and squirrel-proof them if possible!

What food would appeal to backyard birds?

Black oil sunflower seeds will attract birds such as grosbeaks and chickadees. Smaller seeds, like millet, will encourage nuthatches and finches. Birds that need high energy foods, like woodpeckers, will head straight to a suet cake, and nectar might tempt hummingbirds into your garden. Jays and magpies adore unsalted peanuts, and chunks of fruit are a favorite with orioles.

Can I make my own suet cake?

Sure! Here's what you need:

Empty, clean yogurt cups · a pencil or pen · a mixing bowl · scissors · suet or lard (butter-like fat) · a butter knife · things birds would eat, including good-quality bird seed, raisins, unsalted peanuts, and grated cheese

(Important! This recipe is not for kids who are allergic to nuts. Keep raisins away from dogs and cats. Don't eat any bird seed, peanuts, or other food you buy specifically for birds!)

1. Using a pencil or pen, poke a small hole in the base of the yogurt cup. (Get an adult to help if needed!) Pull your string through the hole, and tie a big knot on the inside. Make sure the string is long enough to tie the cup to a bird feeder or branch, then use the scissors to trim the string.

2. Once the suet or lard is at room temperature, use the butter knife to cut it into small pieces. Put these pieces into the bowl.

3. Add the other ingredients bit by bit, and mix them up with your fingers until they all hold together.

4. Fill the yogurt cups with the mixture. Place them in the refrigerator for at least an hour to harden.

5. After taking them out of the fridge, separate the cake and cup. Pull the cup up and off the string. Hang the cake from a tree or bird feeder, and wait for the birds to arrive!

Do birds need water?

A bird bath would be a great way to attract more species to your backyard. Even better: Add a fountain or water feature. Birds are intrigued by the sound of moving water, so they'll come and check it out! Keep your bird bath clean.

How can I keep the birds safe?

Birds need safety, so having some shelter in your garden will encourage even timid species to swoop by. Birds can find cover under plants and shrubs, in a brush pile, or in a roost box. If you add a birdhouse, birds may nest in it. You can give breeding birds a helping hand by providing nest materials such as string, hair, pet fur, and yarn.

How can I spot and identify birds?
Simply look out of the window, head into your backyard, or take a trip to a park, beach, forest, or lake. (Go with an adult and check that you have permission to be there.)

Stay extra quiet and still. Look on the ground, in the sky, and in the trees.

Listen! You can spot birds with your ears, too. Many websites have bird song audio guides, which will help you identify the bird sounds you hear.

After some practice, you could try using binoculars to see a bird close-up.

What do you call two birds that are stuck together?

Vel-crows!

You can recognize birds by looking at their:

- Size and shape
- Color and pattern
- Behavior
- Habitat and environment

Look for any markings that stand out, like a ring of color around the eye or a colored bar on the wing. Is the bird perching on a tree branch, wading in a stream, or soaring very high in the air? Is it eating something? Moving in an unusual way? Fighting or chatting with another bird? All of these clues will tell you more about the bird and how it lives!

Good luck! You're ready for take-off!

CHECK OUT ALL OF THE FANTASTIC FACTS IN THIS SENSATIONAL SERIES!